Fadi's Cooking Book

25 Intercultural Recipes, Tips & Techniques

By Fadi Murtada

Table of Contents

Introduction

Welcome to "Fadi's Cooking Book" Here you will discover a diverse collection of recipes from around the world that celebrate the rich and delicious cultural heritage of different countries.

From aromatic biryanis from India to juicy tacos al pastor from Mexico, we take you on a culinary journey through the vibrant flavors and unique ingredients of different cultures. Each recipe is carefully crafted to bring authentic tastes to your kitchen and create an experience that will awaken your senses and awaken your love of cooking.

Whether you're an experienced cook or just starting out, this is the perfect resource for exploring new cuisines and expanding your culinary knowledge. With easy-to-follow instructions and a wide range of recipes to choose from, you'll have everything you need to create delicious and authentic dishes that will impress your friends and family.

So, whether you're looking to spice up your meal routine, or just want to broaden your horizons, our intercultural cooking guide is perfect for a culinary

adventure. So let's start cooking!

Fadi's recipes

Colcannon Potatoes

Ingredients:

- 2 lbs. potatoes, peeled and chopped
- 1/2 cup milk
- 1/4 cup butter
- 1/2 onion, chopped

- 2 cloves garlic, minced
- 2 cups kale, chopped
- 1/2 cup heavy cream
- Salt and pepper to taste

Preparation:

1. Boil the potatoes in a large pot of salted water for 20-25 minutes or until tender.
2. Drain the potatoes and return them to the pot.
3. Mash the potatoes with the milk and butter until smooth.
4. In a large pan, heat 1 tablespoon of oil over medium heat.
5. Add the onion and garlic and cook until softened, about 5 minutes.
6. Add the kale and cook until wilted, about 2-3 minutes.
7. Stir in the heavy cream and cook until heated through.
8. Season with salt and pepper to taste.
9. Stir the kale mixture into the mashed potatoes.
10. Serve hot, garnished with additional butter and chopped fresh parsley if desired.

Additional notes:

- You can also add chopped cooked bacon for extra flavor.
- For a lighter version, replace the heavy cream with milk or non-dairy milk.
- You can also use collard greens or Swiss chard instead of kale.
- Serve with roasted or grilled meats or as a side dish for any meal.

English Rhubarb Crumble

Ingredients:

- 4 cups rhubarb, chopped
- 1 cup sugar
- 2 tablespoons cornstarch
- 1 teaspoon ground cinnamon
- 1/2 teaspoon ground nutmeg
- 1/2 cup all-purpose flour
- 1/2 cup rolled oats
- 1/2 cup packed brown sugar
- 1/2 cup unsalted butter, chilled and cubed
- 1/2 cup chopped walnuts

Preparation:

1. Preheat the oven to 375°F (190°C).
2. In a large bowl, mix together the rhubarb, sugar, cornstarch, cinnamon, and nutmeg.
3. Pour the mixture into a 9x9-inch baking dish.
4. In a separate bowl, mix together the flour, oats, brown sugar, and butter.
5. Stir in the chopped walnuts.
6. Sprinkle the mixture over the rhubarb mixture in the baking dish.
7. Bake for 35-40 minutes, or until the topping is golden brown and the rhubarb is tender.
8. Serve warm with vanilla ice cream or whipped cream.

Additional notes:

- You can also add diced apples or other fruit to the mixture for a mixed fruit crumble.
- For a gluten-free version, use gluten-free flour and oats.
- If the crumble is too sweet, reduce the amount of sugar in the topping.
- This dish can be made ahead of time and reheated before serving.

German Potato Dumplings

Ingredients:

- 2 lbs. potatoes, peeled and grated
- 1 egg
- 1/2 cup all-purpose flour
- 2 teaspoons salt
- 1/4 teaspoon black pepper
- 2 tablespoons butter
- 2 tablespoons breadcrumbs

Preparation:

1. In a large bowl, mix together the grated potatoes, egg, flour, salt, and pepper until a dough forms.
2. Shape the dough into 8-10 balls.
3. Bring a large pot of salted water to a boil.
4. Gently place the dumplings into the boiling water and cook for 10-12 minutes, or until they float to the surface.
5. Drain the dumplings and transfer them to a serving dish.
6. In a small saucepan, melt the butter and stir in the breadcrumbs.
7. Spoon the breadcrumb mixture over the dumplings and serve hot with gravy or sautéed mushrooms.

Additional notes:

- For a lighter version, you can steam the dumplings instead of boiling them.
- Serve the dumplings with roasted meats, sauerkraut, or red cabbage.
- If the dough is too sticky, add more flour until it is easier to handle.

Aebleskiver

Ingredients:

- 2 cups all-purpose flour
- 2 teaspoons baking powder
- 1/2 teaspoon baking soda
- 1/2 teaspoon salt
- 1/4 teaspoon ground cardamom
- 1/4 teaspoon ground nutmeg
- 3 eggs, separated
- 2 cups buttermilk
- 2 tablespoons sugar

- 4 tablespoons unsalted butter, melted

Preparation:

1. In a large bowl, whisk together the flour, baking powder, baking soda, salt, cardamom, and nutmeg.
2. In a separate bowl, beat the egg whites until stiff peaks form.
3. In another bowl, mix together the egg yolks, buttermilk, sugar, and melted butter.
4. Stir the buttermilk mixture into the flour mixture until just combined.
5. Gently fold in the egg whites.
6. Heat an aebleskiver pan over medium heat.
7. Grease each well with a small amount of oil or butter.
8. Fill each well about 3/4 full with batter.
9. Cook until the edges are set and the bottom is golden brown, about 2 minutes.
10. Use a skewer or toothpick to flip each aebleskiver and cook until the other side is golden brown, about 1-2 minutes more.
11. Serve hot with powdered sugar and jam or syrup.

Additional notes:

- Aebleskiver pans can be found in specialty kitchen stores or online.

- You can also add fillings such as fruit, nutella, or cheese to the batter before cooking.

- For a sweeter version, add more sugar to the batter.

- Serve as a breakfast dish or as a dessert with ice cream.

Hazelnut Macarons

Ingredients:

- 200 grams almond flour
- 200 grams powdered sugar
- 100 grams egg whites (from about 3-4 eggs), room temperature
- 50 grams granulated sugar
- 1 teaspoon vanilla extract
- 50 grams hazelnut paste
- Green food coloring (optional)
- 200 grams dark chocolate, melted

Preparation:

1. Line two baking sheets with parchment paper.
2. In a food processor, pulse the almond flour and powdered sugar until combined. Sift the mixture into a large bowl.
3. In a separate bowl, beat the egg whites until foamy.
4. Slowly add the granulated sugar and beat until stiff peaks form.
5. Stir in the vanilla extract and food coloring, if using.
6. Fold the egg white mixture into the almond flour mixture until just combined.
7. Spoon the mixture into a piping bag fitted with a round tip.
8. Pipe 1 1/2-inch rounds onto the prepared baking sheets, spacing them about 1 inch apart.
9. Let the macarons sit at room temperature for 30 minutes to an hour, or until a skin forms on the surface.
10. Preheat the oven to 300°F (150°C).
11. Bake the macarons for 12-15 minutes, or until the feet are formed and the tops are set.
12. Let the macarons cool completely on the baking sheets.
13. Spread a small amount of hazelnut paste onto half of the macarons.

14. Spoon the melted chocolate into a piping bag and pipe a small amount onto the remaining macarons.

15. Sandwich the chocolate and hazelnut macarons together.

16. Serve at room temperature or store in an airtight container in the refrigerator for up to 3 days.

Additional notes:

- Macarons are finicky to make and may take a few tries to perfect. Be sure to follow the steps carefully and measure the ingredients precisely.

- The macarons can also be filled with different flavors of buttercream, ganache, or jam.

- For a nut-free version, use almond extract instead of hazelnut paste and substitute the almond flour with ground oats.

- For a gluten-free version, make sure to use gluten-free powdered sugar.

Crispy Norwegian Bows

Ingredients:

- 4 cups all-purpose flour

- 1 teaspoon salt

- 1 teaspoon sugar

- 1 teaspoon active dry yeast

- 1 3/4 cups warm water

- 1/2 cup butter, melted

- 1 egg, beaten

- Coarse sea salt, for sprinkling

Preparation:

1. In a large bowl, mix together the flour, salt, sugar, and yeast.
2. Gradually add in the warm water, stirring until a sticky dough forms.
3. Knead the dough on a floured surface for 5 minutes, or until it is smooth and elastic.
4. Place the dough in a greased bowl, cover with plastic wrap, and let it rise in a warm place for 1 hour, or until doubled in size.
5. Preheat the oven to 400°F (200°C). Line a baking sheet with parchment paper.
6. Divide the dough into 8 equal pieces and roll each piece into a long rope.
7. Take the ends of each rope and cross them over each other, making a bow shape.
8. Place the bows onto the prepared baking sheet and brush with the beaten egg.
9. Sprinkle with coarse sea salt.
10. Bake for 15-20 minutes, or until golden brown.
11. Remove from the oven and brush with melted butter.
12. Serve warm.

Additional notes:

- Norwegian bows are a popular snack in Norway, often served as an accompaniment to soup or a main dish.

- For a sweeter version, sprinkle the bows with cinnamon sugar before baking.

- The bows can also be filled with cheese or ham before baking for a savory twist.

- Store the bows in an airtight container at room temperature for up to 2 days. To reheat, place them in a 350°F (175°C) oven for 5 minutes, or until warm.

Swedish Cream Apple Rings

Ingredients:

- 2 large apples, cored and sliced into 1/2 inch rounds
- 1/2 cup all-purpose flour
- 1/2 cup sugar
- 1/2 teaspoon ground cinnamon
- 1/4 teaspoon ground nutmeg
- 1/4 teaspoon ground ginger
- 1/4 teaspoon baking powder
- 1/4 teaspoon baking soda
- 1/2 cup sour cream

- 1 egg
- 1 teaspoon vanilla extract
- 1/2 cup heavy cream
- 1/4 cup confectioners' sugar

Preparation:

1. Preheat the oven to 400°F (200°C). Line a baking sheet with parchment paper.
2. In a bowl, mix together the flour, sugar, cinnamon, nutmeg, ginger, baking powder, and baking soda.
3. In another bowl, mix together the sour cream, egg, and vanilla extract.
4. Add the dry ingredients to the wet ingredients and mix until just combined.
5. Dip each apple slice into the batter, allowing the excess to drip off.
6. Place the apple slices onto the prepared baking sheet and bake for 15-20 minutes, or until golden brown.
7. In a large bowl, beat the heavy cream and confectioners' sugar until soft peaks form.

8. Serve the apple rings with a dollop of whipped cream on top.

Additional notes:

- Swedish cream apple rings are a traditional dessert in Sweden, typically served during the holiday season.
- For a sweeter version, sprinkle the apple rings with additional sugar before baking.
- The apple rings can also be topped with caramel sauce or a scoop of vanilla ice cream.
- Store the apple rings in an airtight container in the refrigerator for up to 2 days. To reheat, place them in a 350°F (175°C) oven for 5 minutes, or until warm.

Steamed Mussels with Peppers

Ingredients:

- 2 lbs mussels, scrubbed and debearded
- 3 tablespoons olive oil
- 2 red bell peppers, seeded and diced
- 2 green bell peppers, seeded and diced
- 4 cloves garlic, minced
- 1/2 cup white wine
- 1/2 cup chicken or vegetable broth
- 1/4 teaspoon red pepper flakes
- 1/4 cup chopped fresh parsley
- Salt and black pepper, to taste

Preparation:

1. In a large pot or Dutch oven, heat the olive oil over medium heat.
2. Add the red and green bell peppers and cook until they are soft and slightly caramelized, about 10 minutes.
3. Add the garlic and cook for another minute.
4. Pour in the wine, broth, and red pepper flakes, and bring to a boil.
5. Add the mussels to the pot, cover, and steam until they open, about 5 minutes. Discard any mussels that do not open.
6. Stir in the parsley and season with salt and black pepper to taste.
7. Serve the mussels with the pepper mixture and some crusty bread for dipping in the broth.

Additional notes:

- Steamed mussels with peppers is a classic French dish that is quick and easy to prepare.
- The dish can also be made with other types of seafood, such as clams or scallops.
- For a creamier version, stir in a few spoonfuls of heavy cream before serving.

- The mussels can also be served over pasta, rice, or mashed potatoes.
- Store any leftovers in an airtight container in the refrigerator for up to 2 days. To reheat, place them in a pot and heat until warm, stirring occasionally.

Shrimp Mozambique

Ingredients:

- 1 pound of large shrimp, peeled and deveined
- 2 tablespoons olive oil
- 4 cloves of garlic, minced
- 1 large onion, chopped
- 1 red bell pepper, sliced
- 1 green bell pepper, sliced
- 1 cup of canned diced tomatoes
- 1 teaspoon paprika
- 1 teaspoon dried oregano
- 1 teaspoon dried thyme

- 1 teaspoon cayenne pepper

- 1/2 teaspoon salt

- 1/2 teaspoon black pepper

- 1/2 cup white wine

- 1/4 cup lemon juice

- 1/4 cup chopped fresh parsley

Preparation:

1. Heat the olive oil in a large skillet over medium heat.
2. Add the garlic and onion, cook for 2-3 minutes until softened.
3. Add the red and green bell pepper, cook for 2-3 minutes until slightly softened.
4. Add the diced tomatoes, paprika, oregano, thyme, cayenne pepper, salt, and black pepper. Stir well.
5. Add the white wine and lemon juice and bring the mixture to a boil.
6. Reduce heat to medium-low and let simmer for 5 minutes.
7. Add the shrimp to the skillet, cover, and cook for 4-5 minutes until the shrimp are pink and cooked through.
8. Sprinkle with fresh parsley and serve immediately.

Additional Notes:

- Serve Shrimp Mozambique over a bed of white rice or with crusty bread to soak up the delicious sauce.
- Feel free to adjust the amount of cayenne pepper to your liking.

Cuccidati

Ingredients:

- 1 pound of dates, pitted and chopped
- 1 pound of dried figs, chopped
- 1/2 pound of raisins
- 1/2 pound of walnuts, chopped
- 1/2 cup of orange juice
- 1/2 cup of brandy
- 1 teaspoon ground cinnamon
- 1/4 teaspoon ground cloves
- 1/4 teaspoon ground nutmeg
- 1/4 teaspoon salt

- 1 cup of all-purpose flour

- 1/2 cup of sugar

- 1/2 cup of unsalted butter, room temperature

- 1 large egg

- 1 teaspoon vanilla extract

- Confectioners' sugar for dusting (optional)

Preparation:

1. Preheat your oven to 350°F. Line a baking sheet with parchment paper.

2. In a large saucepan, combine the chopped dates, figs, raisins, walnuts, orange juice, brandy, cinnamon, cloves, nutmeg, and salt. Cook over medium heat until the fruit is soft and the liquid has been absorbed, about 10 minutes.

3. In a separate bowl, cream the butter and sugar until light and fluffy.

4. Beat in the egg and vanilla extract.

5. Gradually add the flour to the mixture, mixing until just combined.

6. Stir in the cooked fruit mixture.

7. Using a cookie scoop or tablespoon, drop spoonfuls of the dough onto the prepared baking sheet.

8. Bake for 15-20 minutes, or until the edges are lightly golden.

9. Cool on a wire rack.

10. Dust with confectioners' sugar before serving, if
   desired.

Additional Notes:

- Cuccidati is a traditional Italian cookie that is typically enjoyed during the holiday season.
- You can also add in additional ingredients like almonds, hazelnuts, or chocolate chips to the fruit mixture.
- For a smoother filling, you can pulse the fruit mixture in a food processor before adding it to the cookie dough.
- Cuccidati can be stored in an airtight container for up to a week.

Chicken Yakitori

Ingredients:

- 1 pound of boneless, skinless chicken thighs, cut into 1-inch pieces
- 1/4 cup of soy sauce
- 1/4 cup of sake or rice wine
- 2 tablespoons of mirin (sweet cooking sake)
- 2 tablespoons of brown sugar
- 2 cloves of garlic, minced
- 1 inch piece of ginger, grated

- 8-10 bamboo skewers, soaked in water for 30 minutes

Preparation:

1. In a small saucepan, combine the soy sauce, sake, mirin, brown sugar, garlic, and ginger.
2. Heat the mixture over medium heat until the sugar has dissolved.
3. Remove from heat and let cool.
4. Thread the chicken pieces onto the soaked bamboo skewers.
5. Heat your grill or grill pan to medium-high heat.
6. Brush the chicken with the sauce and grill for 5-7 minutes on each side, until fully cooked and slightly charred.
7. Brush with additional sauce during grilling, if desired.
8. Serve with steamed rice and vegetables, if desired.

Additional Notes:

- You can also use boneless, skinless chicken breast for this recipe, but keep in mind that chicken thighs tend to be more flavorful and moist.
- If you don't have sake or mirin, you can substitute with a dry white wine or rice vinegar.

- Be sure to soak the bamboo skewers in water before using to prevent them from burning on the grill.

Sour Cream Cucumbers

Ingredients:

- 4 medium cucumbers, sliced
- 1/2 teaspoon salt
- 1/2 teaspoon black pepper
- 1/2 cup of sour cream
- 2 tablespoons of white wine vinegar
- 1 tablespoon of sugar
- 1 tablespoon of chopped fresh dill
- 1 clove of garlic, minced

Preparation:

1. In a colander, toss the sliced cucumbers with the salt and let sit for 10-15 minutes.
2. Rinse the cucumbers with cold water and pat dry.
3. In a small bowl, whisk together the sour cream, white wine vinegar, sugar, dill, and garlic.
4. In a large bowl, combine the cucumbers and the sour cream mixture.
5. Toss to evenly coat.
6. Cover and refrigerate for at least 30 minutes, or up to 2 hours, to allow the flavors to develop.
7. Serve chilled as a side dish or as a light and refreshing snack.

Additional Notes:

- For a tangier flavor, you can add more vinegar or lemon juice to the sour cream mixture.
- You can also add sliced red onion or diced red bell pepper for additional color and flavor.
- If you prefer a smoother consistency, you can puree the sour cream mixture in a blender or food processor.

- Leftovers can be stored in the refrigerator for up to 3 days, but the cucumbers may release more liquid and become softer over time.

Coconut-Mango Malva Pudding

Ingredients:

- 1 cup of self-raising flour
- 1 cup of sugar
- 1 cup of coconut milk
- 1/2 cup of melted butter
- 2 eggs
- 1 teaspoon of white vinegar
- 1 teaspoon of vanilla extract
- 1 ripe mango, peeled and diced
- 1/2 cup of heavy cream

- 1/2 cup of shredded coconut

Preparation:

1. Preheat your oven to 350°F (175°C).
2. Grease a 9x9 inch baking dish.
3. In a large bowl, whisk together the flour and sugar.
4. In a separate bowl, whisk together the coconut milk, melted butter, eggs, vinegar, and vanilla extract.
5. Pour the wet ingredients into the dry ingredients and mix until just combined.
6. Pour the batter into the prepared baking dish.
7. Sprinkle the diced mango and shredded coconut over the batter.
8. Bake for 35-40 minutes, or until a toothpick inserted in the center comes out clean.
9. In a large bowl, whip the heavy cream until stiff peaks form.
10. Serve the warm pudding topped with the whipped cream and additional mango and coconut, if desired.

Additional Notes:

- You can substitute self-raising flour with all-purpose flour and add 1 teaspoon of baking powder.
- If you prefer a sweeter pudding, you can add more sugar to the batter.

- You can also use canned coconut milk, but make sure to shake the can well before using.

- Malva pudding is traditionally served warm, but you can also enjoy it chilled.

- Leftovers can be stored in the refrigerator for up to 3 days.

Malfouf Recipe

Ingredients:

- 1 head of green cabbage, sliced
- 3 tablespoons of olive oil
- 2 medium onions, chopped
- 2 cloves of garlic, minced
- 1 teaspoon of ground cumin
- 1 teaspoon of paprika
- 1/2 teaspoon of allspice
- 1/2 teaspoon of cinnamon
- Salt and black pepper, to taste
- 1 cup of long-grain rice

- 2 cups of water

- 1/2 cup of lemon juice

- 1/4 cup of chopped fresh parsley

- 1/4 cup of chopped fresh mint

Preparation:

1. In a large saucepan, heat the olive oil over medium heat.
2. Add the onions and garlic and cook until softened, about 5 minutes.
3. Stir in the cumin, paprika, allspice, cinnamon, salt, and pepper.
4. Add the rice and stir to coat.
5. Add the water and bring to a boil.
6. Reduce the heat to low, cover, and simmer for 18-20 minutes, or until the water has been absorbed and the rice is cooked.
7. Stir in the lemon juice, parsley, and mint.
8. In a large bowl, combine the cabbage and the cooked rice mixture.
9. Toss to evenly mix.
10. Serve warm or at room temperature as a side dish or main course.

Additional Notes:

- You can also add chopped tomatoes, diced carrots, or chopped nuts to the dish for added texture and flavor.
- If you prefer a sweeter dish, you can add more lemon juice or honey to the recipe.
- For a vegetarian version, you can substitute vegetable broth for the water.
- Malfouf can be stored in the refrigerator for up to 3 days, but it is best served fresh.

Lahmajoun (Armenian Pizza)

Ingredients:

- 1 pound of ground beef
- 2 medium onions, minced
- 3 cloves of garlic, minced
- 1 teaspoon of ground cumin
- 1 teaspoon of paprika
- Salt and black pepper, to taste
- 1/4 cup of tomato paste
- 1/4 cup of water

- 2 pita breads

- 1 cup of shredded mozzarella cheese

- 1/4 cup of chopped fresh parsley

Preparation:

1. Preheat your oven to 400°F (200°C).
2. In a large skillet, cook the ground beef over medium heat until browned, about 10 minutes.
3. Add the onions and garlic and cook until softened, about 5 minutes.
4. Stir in the cumin, paprika, salt, and pepper.
5. In a small bowl, whisk together the tomato paste and water.
6. Stir the tomato paste mixture into the beef mixture.
7. Remove from heat and let the mixture cool.
8. Place the pita breads on a baking sheet.
9. Spoon the beef mixture over the pita breads, spreading it evenly.
10. Sprinkle the mozzarella cheese over the beef mixture.
11. Bake for 10-15 minutes, or until the cheese is melted and bubbly.
12. Sprinkle the parsley over the pizzas.
13. Serve warm.

Additional Notes:

- You can also add chopped olives, diced bell peppers, or other toppings of your choice to the pizzas.
- If you prefer a spicier flavor, you can add more paprika or chili powder to the beef mixture.
- For a vegetarian version, you can substitute the ground beef with diced mushrooms or other vegetables.
- Lahmajoun can be stored in the refrigerator for up to 3 days, but it is best served fresh.

Beef & Onion Piroshki

Ingredients:

- 1 pound of ground beef
- 2 medium onions, chopped
- 3 cloves of garlic, minced
- 1 teaspoon of dried thyme
- Salt and black pepper, to taste
- 2 tablespoons of all-purpose flour
- 2 tablespoons of butter
- 1 cup of beef broth
- 2 tablespoons of sour cream
- 2 sheets of puff pastry, thawed

- 1 egg, beaten

- Sesame seeds, for garnish

Preparation:

1. Preheat your oven to 400°F (200°C).
2. In a large skillet, cook the ground beef over medium heat until browned, about 10 minutes.
3. Add the onions and garlic and cook until softened, about 5 minutes.
4. Stir in the thyme, salt, and pepper.
5. Sprinkle the flour over the beef mixture and stir to combine.
6. Add the butter and stir until melted.
7. Gradually pour in the beef broth, stirring constantly.
8. Bring the mixture to a simmer and cook until thickened, about 5 minutes.
9. Remove from heat and stir in the sour cream.
10. Roll out the puff pastry on a lightly floured surface.
11. Cut the pastry into 4-inch squares.
12. Spoon the beef mixture onto one half of each square.
13. Fold the other half of the square over the filling to form a triangle.
14. Place the piroshkis on a baking sheet.
15. Brush the tops with the beaten egg.
16. Sprinkle the sesame seeds over the piroshkis.

17. Bake for 15-20 minutes, or until the pastry is golden
    brown.

18. Serve warm.

Additional Notes:

- You can also add diced carrots, mushrooms, or other
  vegetables to the beef mixture.

- If you prefer a spicier flavor, you can add a pinch of
  cayenne pepper or chili powder to the beef mixture.

- For a vegetarian version, you can substitute the
  ground beef with diced potatoes, lentils, or other
  vegetables.

- Piroshkis can be stored in the refrigerator for up to 2
  days, but they are best served fresh.

Chicken Tikka Masala

Ingredients:

- 4 boneless, skinless chicken breasts, cut into bite-sized pieces
- 1 cup of plain yogurt
- 2 tablespoons of lemon juice
- 2 teaspoons of garam masala
- 1 teaspoon of cumin
- 1 teaspoon of paprika
- 1 teaspoon of turmeric
- 1 teaspoon of coriander
- 1 teaspoon of cayenne pepper (optional)
- Salt and black pepper, to taste

- 2 tablespoons of vegetable oil
- 2 medium onions, minced
- 4 cloves of garlic, minced
- 1-inch piece of ginger, grated
- 1 can of diced tomatoes (14 oz)
- 1 cup of heavy cream
- Fresh cilantro, for garnish

Preparation:

1. In a large bowl, mix together the chicken, yogurt, lemon juice, garam masala, cumin, paprika, turmeric, coriander, cayenne pepper (if using), salt, and pepper.
2. Cover and refrigerate for at least 30 minutes or up to 2 hours.
3. In a large skillet, heat the oil over medium heat.
4. Add the onions, garlic, and ginger and cook until softened, about 5 minutes.
5. Stir in the diced tomatoes and bring to a simmer.
6. Reduce the heat to low and let the mixture cook for 10 minutes.
7. Stir in the heavy cream and let the mixture simmer for another 5 minutes.
8. Add the chicken to the sauce and stir to combine.
9. Cover and let the chicken simmer until fully cooked, about 15-20 minutes.
10. Serve over rice, garnished with fresh cilantro.

Additional Notes:

- You can also add diced bell peppers, mushrooms, or other vegetables to the sauce.
- If you prefer a spicier flavor, you can add more cayenne pepper or chili powder to the sauce.
- For a vegetarian version, you can substitute the chicken with diced tofu, eggplant, or other vegetables.
- Chicken Tikka Masala can be stored in the refrigerator for up to 3 days, but it is best served fresh.

Mango Lassi

Ingredients:

- 2 ripe mangoes, peeled and diced
- 1 cup of plain yogurt
- 1/2 cup of cold water
- 2 tablespoons of sugar (or to taste)
- 1/2 teaspoon of cardamom powder
- Ice cubes (optional)

Preparation:

1. In a blender, puree the mangoes until smooth.
2. Add the yogurt, water, sugar, and cardamom powder and blend until well combined.

3. Taste and adjust the sweetness as needed.

4. If desired, add a few ice cubes and blend until
    smooth.

5. Pour into glasses and serve immediately.

Additional Notes:

- If you prefer a thicker consistency, you can add more
  yogurt or a few more ice cubes.

- You can also substitute the sugar with honey or agave
  syrup.

- For a vegan version, you can use a plant-based yogurt
  or coconut cream instead of dairy yogurt.

- Mango Lassi can be stored in the refrigerator for up
  to 2 days, but it is best served fresh.

Vegetable Pad Thai

Ingredients:

- 8 oz. dried rice noodles
- 3 tablespoons of vegetable oil
- 3 cloves of garlic, minced
- 1 large red bell pepper, sliced into thin strips
- 1 large yellow onion, sliced
- 1 cup of sliced mushrooms
- 1 cup of bean sprouts
- 2 large carrots, julienned
- 2 large eggs, lightly beaten
- 3 tablespoons of soy sauce

- 2 tablespoons of brown sugar
- 2 tablespoons of rice vinegar
- 2 tablespoons of freshly squeezed lime juice
- 1 teaspoon of chili flakes (optional)
- 1/4 cup of chopped peanuts
- Fresh cilantro and lime wedges, for garnish

Preparation:

1. Soak the rice noodles in warm water for 10-15 minutes, or until softened. Drain and set aside.
2. In a large wok or skillet, heat the oil over high heat.
3. Add the garlic and cook for 30 seconds, or until fragrant.
4. Add the bell pepper, onion, mushrooms, bean sprouts, and carrots and stir-fry for 3-5 minutes, or until vegetables are tender but still crisp.
5. Push the vegetables to the side of the pan and add the beaten eggs to the center. Scramble until cooked, then stir into the vegetables.
6. Add the noodles, soy sauce, brown sugar, rice vinegar, lime juice, and chili flakes (if using) to the pan and stir-fry until everything is well combined and heated through, about 3-5 minutes.
7. Serve hot, topped with chopped peanuts, fresh cilantro, and a lime wedge on the side.

Additional Notes:

- You can add or substitute other vegetables as desired, such as broccoli, snow peas, or zucchini.
- If you prefer a spicier flavor, you can add more chili flakes or a splash of sriracha sauce.
- For a vegan version, you can use a plant-based protein, such as tofu or tempeh, in place of the eggs.
- Vegetable Pad Thai can be stored in the refrigerator for up to 2 days, but it is best served fresh.

Chinese Scallion Pancakes

Ingredients:

- 2 cups of all-purpose flour
- 1/2 teaspoon of salt
- 1/2 cup of boiling water
- 1/2 cup of cold water
- 1/2 cup of thinly sliced scallions (green onions)
- 2 tablespoons of vegetable oil, plus more for brushing

Preparation:

1. In a large mixing bowl, whisk together the flour and salt.

2. Gradually add the boiling water, stirring constantly until a dough forms.

3. Knead the dough for about 5 minutes, or until smooth and elastic.

4. Cover the dough with plastic wrap and let it rest for 30 minutes.

5. Divide the dough into 8 equal pieces. Roll each piece into a ball and flatten into a disc.

6. On a floured surface, roll out each disc into a thin circle.

7. Brush each circle with oil and sprinkle with sliced scallions.

8. Roll up each circle into a tight spiral, then gently flatten and shape into a round pancake.

9. In a large non-stick skillet, heat 2 tablespoons of oil over medium heat.

10. Cook the pancakes for 2-3 minutes on each side, or until golden brown and crispy.

11. Serve hot, with extra oil for dipping, if desired.

Additional Notes:

- You can add other seasonings, such as ginger, sesame seeds, or chili flakes, to the dough for extra flavor.
- For a gluten-free version, you can use a gluten-free flour blend instead of all-purpose flour.

- • Chinese Scallion Pancakes can be stored in the
  refrigerator for up to 2 days, but they are best served
  fresh and hot.

Vietnamese Pork Lettuce Wraps

Ingredients:

- 1 lb ground pork
- 1/4 cup diced onion
- 2 cloves garlic, minced
- 1 tablespoon soy sauce
- 1 tablespoon fish sauce
- 2 tablespoons hoisin sauce
- 1 tablespoon sugar
- 2 teaspoons cornstarch
- 1 teaspoon sesame oil
- 2 tablespoons vegetable oil
- 1/4 cup diced carrots

- 1/4 cup diced mushrooms

- 1/4 cup diced water chestnuts

- 1/4 cup diced red bell pepper

- 1 head of butter lettuce

- Fresh mint, cilantro, and basil leaves, for garnish

- Sriracha sauce and lime wedges, for serving

Preparation:

1. In a bowl, mix together the ground pork, onion, garlic, soy sauce, fish sauce, hoisin sauce, sugar, and cornstarch.
2. In a large skillet, heat the vegetable oil over medium-high heat. Add the pork mixture to the skillet and cook, breaking it up into small pieces, until browned and cooked through, about 5 to 7 minutes.
3. Add the carrots, mushrooms, water chestnuts, and red bell pepper to the skillet and cook until the vegetables are tender, about 3 to 5 minutes.
4. To assemble the lettuce wraps, place a spoonful of the pork mixture in the center of a lettuce leaf. Add some mint, cilantro, and basil leaves on top. Roll up the lettuce leaf to enclose the filling. Repeat with the remaining lettuce leaves and filling.
5. Serve the lettuce wraps with sriracha sauce and lime wedges on the side.

Additional Notes:

- You can also add additional vegetables to the filling mixture, such as shredded cabbage or julienned cucumber, for added crunch and flavor.
- For a gluten-free option, use gluten-free hoisin sauce and gluten-free soy sauce.
- To make this dish spicier, add some sliced jalapenos or red chili pepper to the filling mixture.

Korean Sausage Bowl

Ingredients:

- 8 ounces Korean-style sausage, sliced
- 1 large onion, diced
- 2 cloves garlic, minced
- 1 large carrot, diced
- 1 large red bell pepper, diced
- 2 cups cooked white rice
- 1 tablespoon gochujang (Korean chili paste)
- 2 teaspoons soy sauce
- 1 teaspoon sugar

- 1 teaspoon sesame oil
- 1 tablespoon vegetable oil
- Sesame seeds and chopped green onions, for garnish
- Fried eggs, optional

Preparation:

1. In a large skillet, heat the vegetable oil over medium-high heat. Add the sausage and cook until browned and crispy, about 5 to 7 minutes. Remove from the skillet and set aside.
2. In the same skillet, add the onion, garlic, carrot, and red bell pepper and cook until the vegetables are tender, about 3 to 5 minutes.
3. Add the gochujang, soy sauce, sugar, and sesame oil to the skillet and stir to combine.
4. Return the sausage to the skillet and stir to coat with the sauce.
5. In a serving bowl, place a scoop of cooked rice. Spoon the sausage mixture over the rice.
6. Garnish with sesame seeds and chopped green onions. Serve with a fried egg, if desired.

Additional Notes:

- If you can't find Korean-style sausage, you can use any type of fully cooked sausage that you prefer.

- For a gluten-free option, use gluten-free soy sauce.

- If you like a bit of heat, add some diced jalapenos or red chili pepper to the sausage mixture.

- You can also add additional vegetables to the sausage mixture, such as diced zucchini or mushrooms, for added nutrition and flavor.

Zimtsterne

Ingredients:

- 2 1/2 cups almond flour
- 1/2 cup powdered sugar
- 1 1/2 teaspoons ground cinnamon
- 1/4 teaspoon ground cloves
- Pinch of salt
- 2 egg whites
- 1/2 cup granulated sugar
- Confectioners' sugar, for dusting

Preparation:

1. Preheat your oven to 300°F (150°C) and line a baking sheet with parchment paper.
2. In a medium bowl, whisk together the almond flour, powdered sugar, cinnamon, cloves, and salt.
3. In a large bowl, using an electric mixer, beat the egg whites until stiff peaks form. Gradually add the granulated sugar and beat until the mixture is glossy and stiff.
4. Using a spatula, gently fold the dry ingredients into the egg white mixture.
5. Using a star-shaped cookie cutter, cut out the dough and place on the prepared baking sheet.
6. Bake the cookies for 20 to 25 minutes, or until they are dry to the touch.
7. Let the cookies cool completely on the baking sheet.
8. Dust the cooled cookies with confectioners' sugar before serving.

Additional Notes:

- Zimtsterne are best stored in an airtight container for up to one week.
- You can also add a drizzle of melted chocolate on top of the cookies for added flavor.

- For a gluten-free option, make sure to use gluten-free almond flour.

- You can use any other shape of cookie cutter, but the traditional shape for Zimtsterne is a star.

Argentine Lasagna

Ingredients:

- 1 pound ground beef
- 1 large onion, diced
- 2 cloves garlic, minced
- 1 can (14.5 ounces) diced tomatoes
- 1 can (8 ounces) tomato sauce
- 1 teaspoon dried oregano
- 1 teaspoon dried basil
- Salt and pepper, to taste
- 8 to 10 lasagna noodles
- 1 1/2 cups ricotta cheese

- 1 cup grated mozzarella cheese

- 1/2 cup grated Parmesan cheese

- 2 large eggs

- 2 tablespoons olive oil

- Fresh parsley, for garnish

Preparation:

1. Preheat your oven to 375°F (190°C).

2. In a large saucepan, heat the olive oil over medium heat. Add the onion and garlic and cook until soft and translucent, about 5 to 7 minutes.

3. Add the ground beef to the saucepan and cook until browned, breaking up any large clumps with a wooden spoon.

4. Stir in the diced tomatoes, tomato sauce, oregano, basil, salt, and pepper. Reduce heat to low and simmer for 10 minutes.

5. Cook the lasagna noodles according to the package instructions, until al dente. Drain and set aside.

6. In a medium bowl, mix together the ricotta cheese, mozzarella cheese, Parmesan cheese, and eggs.

7. Spread a thin layer of the meat sauce in the bottom of a 9x13 inch baking dish. Top with a layer of lasagna noodles, followed by a layer of the cheese mixture. Repeat the layers until all ingredients are used, ending with a layer of meat sauce on top.

8. Cover the baking dish with aluminum foil and bake for 30 minutes. Remove the foil and bake for an additional 10 minutes, or until the cheese is melted and golden brown.

9. Let the lasagna cool for 10 minutes before slicing and serving. Garnish with fresh parsley.

Additional Notes:

- If you prefer a creamier lasagna, you can also add a cup of heavy cream to the cheese mixture.

- You can also add other ingredients to the meat sauce, such as diced bell peppers, mushrooms, or zucchini.

- For a vegetarian option, omit the ground beef and use a meat substitute or additional vegetables in the sauce.

Pacoca

Ingredients:

- 2 cups cassava flour
- 1/2 cup sugar
- 1/4 teaspoon salt
- 1/2 cup grated cheese (such as Parmesan or provolone)
- 1/2 cup grated coconut
- Vegetable oil, for frying

Preparation:

1. In a large bowl, mix together the cassava flour, sugar, salt, cheese, and coconut.

2.   Shape the mixture into small balls, about the size of a golf ball.

3.   Heat the vegetable oil in a large saucepan over medium heat until hot.

4.   Fry the pacoca balls in the hot oil until golden brown on all sides, about 3 to 5 minutes.

5.   Remove the pacoca balls from the oil with a slotted spoon and place on a paper towel-lined plate to drain excess oil.

6.   Serve the pacoca balls warm as a snack or dessert.

Additional Notes:

- Pacoca is a traditional Brazilian snack and is often served during festivals and celebrations.

- Cassava flour is made from cassava, a starchy root vegetable commonly used in South American cuisine.

- You can also add additional flavorings to the pacoca mixture, such as cinnamon, nutmeg, or vanilla extract.

- For a gluten-free option, make sure to use gluten-free cassava flour.

Quick Tacos al Pastor

Ingredients:

- 1 lb pork shoulder, thinly sliced
- 1/2 onion, chopped
- 1/4 cup pineapple juice
- 1 tbsp chili powder
- 1 tsp ground cumin
- 1 tsp dried oregano
- 1/2 tsp salt
- 1/4 tsp black pepper
- 1/4 cup chopped fresh cilantro

- 8-10 small corn tortillas

- Sliced pineapple (optional)

- Chopped onion (optional)

- Chopped cilantro (optional)

- Lime wedges (optional)

Preparation:

1. In a large bowl, mix together the sliced pork, chopped onion, pineapple juice, chili powder, cumin, oregano, salt, black pepper, and chopped cilantro. Toss until the pork is well-coated in the spice mixture.

2. Heat a large skillet over medium-high heat. Once hot, add the pork mixture to the skillet and cook for 8-10 minutes, or until the pork is browned and cooked through.

3. Warm the corn tortillas by heating them in a dry skillet or directly over a gas flame until they are lightly charred.

4. To assemble the tacos, place a few slices of the cooked pork onto each tortilla. Top with sliced pineapple, chopped onion, and cilantro, if desired. Serve with lime wedges on the side.

Additional notes:

- For a spicier version of these tacos, add some chopped chipotle peppers in adobo sauce to the pork mixture.

- If you don't have fresh pineapple juice on hand, you can use canned pineapple juice instead.

- To make these tacos even quicker, you can use pre-cooked sliced pork or store-bought cooked carnitas and simply season them with the spice mixture before heating them up in the skillet.

Jamaican Chocolate Cookies with Caramel Crème

Ingredients:

- 1 cup all-purpose flour
- 1/2 cup cocoa powder
- 1/2 teaspoon baking soda
- 1/2 teaspoon salt
- 1/2 cup unsalted butter, softened
- 1/2 cup granulated sugar
- 1/2 cup brown sugar
- 1 egg
- 1 teaspoon vanilla extract
- 1/2 cup dark chocolate chips

- 1/2 cup chopped pecans

For the Caramel Crème:

- 1/4 cup unsalted butter
- 1/2 cup brown sugar
- 1/4 cup heavy cream
- 1/2 teaspoon vanilla extract
- 1/4 teaspoon salt

Preparation:

1. Preheat the oven to 350°F (175°C). Line a baking sheet with parchment paper.
2. In a medium bowl, whisk together the flour, cocoa powder, baking soda, and salt.
3. In a large mixing bowl, beat the butter, granulated sugar, and brown sugar until light and fluffy. Add the egg and vanilla extract and mix until well combined.
4. Add the dry ingredients to the butter mixture and stir until just combined. Fold in the dark chocolate chips and chopped pecans.
5. Using a cookie scoop or tablespoon, drop the dough onto the prepared baking sheet, spacing the cookies about 2 inches apart.

6. Bake the cookies for 12-15 minutes, or until the edges are firm and the centers are set. Remove the cookies from the oven and let them cool on the baking sheet for 5 minutes before transferring them to a wire rack to cool completely.

7. While the cookies are cooling, prepare the caramel crème. In a small saucepan, melt the butter over medium heat. Add the brown sugar and whisk until the sugar is dissolved. Add the heavy cream, vanilla extract, and salt and continue to whisk until the mixture is smooth and creamy.

8. Remove the saucepan from the heat and let the caramel cool for a few minutes.

9. Once the cookies are completely cool, use a spoon or piping bag to drizzle the caramel crème over the tops of the cookies.

10. Serve the Jamaican chocolate cookies with caramel crème and enjoy!

Additional Notes:

- For an extra tropical twist, you can add 1/2 cup of shredded coconut to the cookie dough.
- If you prefer your caramel crème to be thicker, let it cool for a bit longer before drizzling it over the cookies.

Calgary Nanaimo Bars

Ingredients: For the base:

- 1/2 cup unsalted butter, melted
- 1/4 cup granulated sugar
- 1/3 cup cocoa powder
- 1 egg, beaten
- 1 teaspoon vanilla extract
- 2 cups graham cracker crumbs
- 1 cup shredded coconut
- 1/2 cup chopped walnuts

For the filling:

- 1/2 cup unsalted butter, softened
- 3 tablespoons custard powder
- 3 cups powdered sugar
- 1/4 cup milk

For the topping:

- 4 ounces semisweet chocolate
- 1 tablespoon unsalted butter

Preparation:

1. Line a 9-inch square baking pan with parchment paper.
2. In a large mixing bowl, combine the melted butter, granulated sugar, cocoa powder, beaten egg, and vanilla extract. Stir until well combined.
3. Add the graham cracker crumbs, shredded coconut, and chopped walnuts to the mixing bowl and stir until everything is well combined.
4. Press the mixture into the prepared baking pan, using a spatula to smooth it out evenly. Chill in the refrigerator for 1 hour.
5. While the base is chilling, make the filling. In a mixing bowl, cream the softened butter and custard powder together until smooth. Gradually add the

powdered sugar and milk, stirring until everything is well combined.

6. Once the base has chilled, spread the filling over the top, using a spatula to smooth it out evenly. Chill in the refrigerator for 1 hour.

7. For the topping, melt the semisweet chocolate and butter together in a double boiler or in the microwave, stirring until smooth.

8. Once the filling has chilled, pour the melted chocolate over the top, using a spatula to smooth it out evenly.

9. Chill the Nanaimo bars in the refrigerator for 1 hour, or until the chocolate topping has set.

10. Once the bars are set, remove them from the pan and cut them into squares. Serve and enjoy!

Additional Notes:

- Calgary Nanaimo Bars are named after the city of Calgary, Alberta, where they are said to have originated.

- To make these bars gluten-free, simply use gluten-free graham cracker crumbs.

- You can also experiment with different flavors for the filling, such as peppermint or coffee. Simply add the desired flavorings in place of the custard powder.

All-American Pie

Ingredients:

For the pie crust:

- 2 1/2 cups all-purpose flour

- 1 teaspoon salt

- 1 tablespoon granulated sugar

- 1 cup unsalted butter, cold and cut into cubes

- 1/4 to 1/2 cup ice water

For the filling:

- 6 cups sliced apples (about 6 medium apples)
- 1/2 cup granulated sugar
- 1/4 cup all-purpose flour
- 1 teaspoon ground cinnamon
- 1/4 teaspoon ground nutmeg
- 1/4 teaspoon salt
- 2 tablespoons unsalted butter

For the topping:

- 1/2 cup all-purpose flour
- 1/2 cup brown sugar
- 1/2 teaspoon ground cinnamon
- 1/4 teaspoon salt
- 1/2 cup unsalted butter, cold and cut into cubes
- 1 cup rolled oats

Preparation:

1. In a large mixing bowl, combine the flour, salt, and granulated sugar for the pie crust. Add the cold butter and use a pastry blender or your hands to cut the butter into the flour mixture until the mixture resembles coarse crumbs.

2. Gradually add the ice water to the flour mixture, stirring with a wooden spoon until the dough comes together. Divide the dough in half, shape each half into a ball, and flatten into disks. Wrap the disks in plastic wrap and refrigerate for at least 30 minutes.

3. Preheat the oven to 375°F (190°C). Roll out one disk of the pie crust and place it in a 9-inch pie dish. Trim the edges and set aside.

4. In a large mixing bowl, combine the sliced apples, granulated sugar, flour, cinnamon, nutmeg, and salt for the filling. Stir until the apples are evenly coated.

5. Pour the apple mixture into the prepared pie crust. Dot the top of the filling with 2 tablespoons of butter.

6. In a separate mixing bowl, combine the flour, brown sugar, cinnamon, and salt for the topping. Add the cold butter and use a pastry blender or your hands to cut the butter into the flour mixture until the mixture resembles coarse crumbs. Stir in the rolled oats.

7. Sprinkle the topping over the apple filling, covering the top of the pie as evenly as possible.

8. Bake the pie for 45-50 minutes, or until the crust is golden brown and the filling is bubbly. If the crust begins to brown too quickly, cover the edges with foil or a pie shield.

9. Allow the pie to cool to room temperature before serving. Serve with a dollop of whipped cream or a scoop of vanilla ice cream, if desired.

Additional Notes:

- All-American Pie is a classic dessert that is perfect for Thanksgiving, but it's also a great choice for any occasion.
- You can experiment with different types of fruit for the filling, such as peaches or berries. Just be sure to adjust the sugar and spices accordingly.
- If you're short on time, you can use a store-bought pie crust instead of making your own from scratch.

Conclusion

I hope you've enjoyed exploring the rich and diverse world of intercultural cooking through these 25 delicious recipes. Through these dishes, we've seen how different cultural traditions have inspired and influenced one another over time, resulting in a vibrant tapestry of global cuisine.

Cooking is not only a way to nourish our bodies, but it can also be a way to explore different cultures, connect with others, and express our creativity. Intercultural cooking offers us a unique opportunity to experience the richness and diversity of food traditions from around the world, and to appreciate the ways in which they have evolved and been adapted over time.

By experimenting with new ingredients, techniques, and flavors, we can expand our culinary horizons and discover new and exciting ways to nourish ourselves and those we care about. We encourage you to take these recipes as a starting point, and to make them your own by adapting them to your tastes and preferences, or by using them as a springboard to create something entirely new and unique.

Through intercultural cooking, we can learn to appreciate and respect the differences that make us all unique. We can connect with others across cultural, linguistic, and geographic boundaries, and celebrate the shared human experience of preparing and sharing food.

At a time when so many forces seem to be dividing us, intercultural cooking is a reminder that there is still so much that unites us. By embracing the diversity of global cuisine, we can learn to appreciate and celebrate the ways in which we are all connected, and to foster a spirit of curiosity, creativity, and compassion.

So, whether you are a seasoned cook or just beginning your culinary journey, we hope these recipes have inspired you to try something new, to expand your horizons, and to connect with the world around you through the universal language of food.

Disclaimer: Before you start cooking any of the meals, please check the ingredients beforehand in case you are allergic! All the nutrition you can obtain from each and every meal depends on the quantity of ingredients you are using!

 Bon appétit!

About the Author

Fadi Murtada developed his passion for cooking and writing in his late teenage-hood. This is the First of his digital books inspired by the trips he had during the summer of 2022. When just a child, reading his summer school books, he was tired of reading boring stories but something opened his vision about the countless possibilities out there – The Fantasy novels. Currently Fadi's fantasy novel is in production. Cooking made his university life a lot of fun, given the circumstances he was in. One thing he loves saying about cooking – "If you are feeling lazy, then find yourself a nice recipe and try something that you cannot find in your own country's stores and markets!". For more info about the author's social life, please visit

Instagram

https://www.instagram.com/fadi_m10/?__coig_restricted=1

Twitter https://twitter.com/Fadi_Murtada10

Facebook https://www.facebook.com/fadi.murtada.10/